SECRETS OF BASEBALL

TOLD BY

BIG LEAGUE PLAYERS

SECRETS OF BASEBALL
TOLD BY
BIG LEAGUE PLAYERS

ROGERS HORNSBY
ADOLFO LUQUE
CHARLES L. HARTNETT
LOU GEHRIG
"PIE" TRAYNOR
TRIS SPEAKER

APPLEWOOD BOOKS
BEDFORD, MASSACHUSETTS

Secrets of Baseball Told by Big League Players comes from material published in 1927 by D. Appleton and Company.

ISBN 1-55709-431-4

10 9 8 7 6 5 4 3 2 1

Library of Congress Cataloging-in-Publication Data
Secrets of baseball told by big league players / Rogers Hornsby . . . [et al.].
       p.   cm.
  Abridged reprint of book originally published: Sprague Pub. Co., 1918.
  ISBN 1-55709-431-4
  1. Baseball.   I. Hornsby, Rogers, 1896-1963.
GV867.S53   1996
796.357—dc20   95-42272
                                          CIP

SECRETS OF BASEBALL

TOLD BY

BIG LEAGUE PLAYERS

SECRETS OF BASEBALL

CHAPTER I

WAIT FOR A GOOD BALL

BY

ROGERS HORNSBY

SECOND BASEMAN

EVERY boy, at one time or another, has known some chap whose high school or college pitching has been phenomenal—who has imposing strike-out and victory records to his credit—but who seems to have nothing at all on the ball when he gets into faster company. Likely you'll remember the case of Owen Carroll.

Carroll, at Holy Cross College, was a pitching sensation for three years. He had every college nine he faced in 1925 completely at his mercy and won every game. In three years of varsity baseball he lost only 2 games and won 49. So when the Detroit Tigers announced that he would play with them on his graduation other big league teams made envious comment.

Carroll was a "flop" in his first tries at big league baseball. He faced Boston before a big crowd eager to see this pitching marvel—and was batted out of the box. He made one or two other starts during the season and never seemed to hit his college stride.

Common sense tells you that Carroll's ability didn't just fade away over night. He was sent by Detroit to the Toronto team for further seasoning, and his fine record there proved that he could make good. For, if he's like others I've known, he has just as good control, and curves, and speed, as he had when he played against amateurs. The difference in his record must lie in some basic difference in the batting methods of the men he faces. What is the difference—what is it that young batters so often do wrong?

We big leaguers think that the major fault with boys' batting is just this: They hit at bad balls.

That isn't the only fault in batting; there are plenty of others that cut down hitters' averages and help along the pitchers' percentages. But it's the one that bothers high school and college fellows most—major leaguers, too. Let's talk about it.

Every boy who can handle a bat knows what the "good ball zone" is. If the ball is over the plate and between your knees and shoulders, it's a strike; if it's high, low or wide it's a ball. The men who govern the rules didn't decide it that way just to be making another regulation.

They had a reason—and the reason was that balls coming within that rectangle are the ones a batter can most easily and accurately hit. Rules protect you, you see, if you let bad ones go by. But everything is against you when you swing at the bad ones; for if you don't miss altogether, you'll probably foul off or hit an easy pop-up or grounder for a sure out.

One season I had an opportunity to watch a sand lot game, and the big right-fielder on one of the teams was a perfect example of what I mean. This fellow had a long, easy swing at the ball, and every move made me think he was a real batter. Then I saw him face the pitcher, and in five times at bat he made only a single. He swung at anything—low balls he liked particularly, but he bit at just about every pitch, no matter how far he had to reach for it. The result was that in spite of his promise he did nothing but foul or hit weakly into the ground. His one hit was a long clean one—and he made it when he swung at a good pitch!

So learn to judge the ball as it comes up to you, and to decide whether it's going to count for or against you if you strike at it. That's the first thing I want batters coming to the St. Louis club to know, and it's a thing anybody can teach himself. Practice every chance you get; see to it that your high school or club team goes through batting workouts just as a big league club does.

And don't think that because nothing depends on it you are free to cut at the bad balls. Unless the pitch is in the good ball zone, your bat shouldn't leave your shoulder.

When you've got that rule down tight, you're ready to go on with your batting training. There are several things every batter must know, and I'll take them up one at a time.

The first one ties up closely with the good ball rule. *Keep your eye on the ball.* I don't have to tell you that you can't connect squarely with the horsehide if you're not watching it every minute. I've seen fellows who looked at the pitcher, at the field, at the runner, at the player through whom they wanted to hit it. That's bad. From the minute the ball leaves the pitcher's hand to the instant it's where you want to hit it—or let it go by—keep your eye on it. Never look away for a second.

Naturalness is an important part of good batting. A good deal is said about correct batting form; but when you've seen the long, free swing of Harry Heilmann, Detroit player who has led the American League in batting several times, and the tremendous wallop of Babe Ruth, and the powerful choke-swing of of Jim Bottomley, first baseman with the St. Louis Cardinals—when you've seen all these and a lot of others and try to analyze them and write down similarities of form, you'll find it pretty hard to do.

4

WAIT FOR A GOOD BALL

The answer is that all of the great batters have their own individual styles—the styles that are easiest, most natural for them. Cultivate, as far as possible, the style of swing and grip that is simplest for you. I don't mean that you should scorn advice from players or coaches who know good batting; frequently their hints will help tremendously. But work in those hints with your own natural batting-habits—make the two work together.

Your stance at the plate should also be just what is easiest for you. Some players stand with feet close together, others with them spread and not on a line. Every good batter faces the plate squarely, so that he can meet the ball when his bat is at the most forceful point in its arc.

Ordinarily I'd advise every batter to learn to "step into the ball" as he bats, rather than to step backward. "Stepping in" means advancing the left foot (if you're a right-handed batter) toward the pitcher as you swing. That increases the power you impart to the bat, and puts you in good position to start your sprint for first if you connect. . . . Even that is not a hide-bound rule, although most batters practice it religiously. An outstanding exception is Al Simmons, the young outfielder with the Philadelphia Athletics who made such a fine record in 1925, his first big league year. Simmons steps back and still gets his hits. But most batters don't.

Where are you going to grip your bat? That's another question that depends largely on individual preference. Of course, there's more power in the free swing with the bat held at its extreme tip; I hold my bat that way, and likely that's the reason I've been able to put a fair share of balls over the fence. But not all good batters use that grip. Jim Bottomley, second high in the National League in 1925, is a choke hitter (that is, he holds his bat about six inches from the tip and so makes his hits on shorter but extremely powerful swings). So are Blades, Toporcer and other good batters on the St. Louis team.

Ty Cobb has a grip different from both of these. He hits from the right side of the plate, with his right hand at the tip of his bat and his left about five inches above. Every fan knows how successful he's found that grip.

You have your position, your grip. The next thing is to meet the ball. I've already told you that your swing must be easy and natural; it must also be powerful. To get the maximum of power, remember three things:

Swing your bat in one horizontal plane.

Meet the ball at the "top" of the swing; time it correctly.

Don't forget the follow-through.

The first rule is easy to understand. If the bat is moving in one plane—that is, if it's circling perfectly level with the ground—it's going to deliver more power against the ball than it would if it were weaving up and down from one level to another. So train yourself to swing the bat exactly on the plane in which you plan to meet the ball.

Second—time the swing properly. That means that you should hear the crack of bat and ball at just the instant the bat's gained its greatest momentum. Timing is a mighty difficult thing to get exactly right; if every batter had it down pat there'd be a big increase in the home run crop. The great batters are the ones who've perfected their timing—old Hans Wagner, Cobb, Ruth, Sisler of the St. Louis Browns, Jacques Fournier of Brooklyn, Frisch of the Giants, and others.

Don't think that, just because I say timing is hard to get exactly right, it can't be learned. You can improve your timing in baseball just as you can in your golf swing, your tennis swing or your football kicking. Practice is the thing. Thevenow, the young shortstop who plays with St. Louis, proved this. Thevenow came to the Cardinals determined to improve his batting, and every chance he got he had somebody pitching to him. He watched his timing, along with the other elements, and by the end of his first season he was a much better batter.

Follow through! Here again comes the parallel to golf, tennis and football. The bat should not stop dead when it hits the ball, nor immediately afterwards. The arc should continue just as it started; the bat should keep on its path while the ball is well on its way. The follow-through is the logical conclusion of the swing, and it's worth a lot of work. I wish every young batter could watch the work of men like Bottomley, or Zack Wheat, the veteran Brooklyn star. It's his vigorous follow-through that takes Babe Ruth off his balance when he swings and misses; and it's the strength of this follow-through that, imparted to the ball when it meets the bat, gives it such long rides. You don't have to lose balance like Ruth, of course. I never fall, although I put a lot of strength and rhythm into my follow-through.

A mighty good way to develop follow-through is to take your bat and practice free swinging—practice the long level arc and the continuation of the swing far around to the front. There's plenty of rhythm in a good baseball swing; try to get it into your own work.

I've told you that you should meet the ball at the "top" of the swing. There are two more things to know about meeting the ball. One is a snap of the wrists that gives to the bat, just at the moment of impact, an added bit of force. Until the moment of this snap, the bat angles backward from your hands; the snap brings it suddenly out to the perpendicular from your body, so that it smacks the ball squarely instead of at an angle.

The second question is that of just where to plan on hitting the ball—directly over the plate and opposite your body, or out in front and slightly ahead of your body. Both methods are used in big league play. Stuffy McInnis, right-handed batter with the Pittsburgh Pirates, hits in front of the plate, as do many others. I hit the ball in closer to my body. It seems to be a question of individual differences again. Ernie Vick —you'll remember his name in football as well as baseball, for he was All-American center at the University of Michigan, as well as a star catcher, before he joined the Cardinals—learned to improve his hitting considerably by connecting out in front of the plate.

Bunting is a form of batting that absolutely demands hitting out in front. Your purpose in a bunt is to lay the ball down where it's going to be hardest for anybody to field. In effect, you stop the ball dead at the plate; your bat doesn't crash into it as in an attempt at a smashing hit, but simply meets it and drops it on the ground at your feet with just enough force to keep it out of the catcher's reach, but not enough to carry it too rapidly to any other fielder.

Since the purpose of the bunt is to stop the ball and put it where it can be fielded with most difficulty the direction in which you send it must be controlled. You must be able to tap it along the third base foul line, or toward the first sacker, or to the pitcher's right if you know he has difficulty in fielding that kind of ball. And in order to control the bunt you must hit it out in front. You can't do it accurately if you try to meet the ball over the plate, even with your body. Some men always step far to the front of the batting box for a bunt.

So keep that in mind when you try to bunt. Remember, too, that you don't get the free swing into a bunt. The bat is almost motionless, as a rule, when it meets the ball. Most players choke their bats when they bunt.

Here's a warning on bunting: Do your best to hide your intentions from the men in the field. Of course, there are plenty of situations when the bunt is a conventional play—when there are less than two down and a man is on first, for instance —and usually in such situations the third baseman and the others will play in. But if you hold your bat in just the same way you do for a full swing, at least until the pitcher delivers the ball, don't look where you're planning to send the ball, and otherwise veil your plans, you've a much better chance of making the bunt effective.

Because bunting is so different from swinging into the ball, it's mighty useful in another way— aiding a batter to work out of a hitting slump. There's never been a very good explanation of a slump—it's something that simply comes. Right in the midst of their season, frequently, leading big league sluggers find themselves unable to connect—their batting eye is bad, their swing feels awkward, their average goes down. Apparently they're doing things properly, too. But the base hits don't come. George Grantham, of the Pittsburgh Pirates, hit the ball hard all season and right up to the World's Series in 1925; he had been particularly effective against right-handed pitchers. But in the Series he couldn't hit a thing —a slump got hold of him.

Often bunting comes in handy in a case like that. When you find you're unable to hit the ball at your usual average, forget every kind of hitting but bunting for a while. Practice all you can on bunting for a few days; gradually work back into regular batting, taking it easy as you go. It's more than likely that you will find the break from free swinging has chased the fault out of your batting, and that you're able to make your share of the hits again.

I've heard high school baseball players exert a lot of extra energy in discussing the virtues of "place hitting." When they get to the big leagues, they'll forget it. Some men, according to report, learn to put the ball where they want it —to smash to left field, or through shortstop, or down a baseline—but I've never run onto any of them.

About the only place hitting we do in the big leagues is try to hit *back* of the runner, rather than in front of him. For instance, if a man is on first and the order is given to sacrifice him to second, a grounder down toward first is a lot more likely to be successful than one toward second. The reason is that he'll be nearer to second than the ball if the ball is hit behind him, and hence have a better chance of getting to his base safely. . . . That's about the extent of place hitting. Spend your time in learning to meet the ball squarely and hit it hard, rather than in trying to place it as you would a tennis ball.

Another question on which young players waste a lot of time is that of figuring what the pitcher is going to do. Is he going to throw a curve? a fast ball? a wide one? And what's the thing to do?

Again I say don't let it bother you. I don't believe in "guess hitting," and never do it myself. Some of the great batters, I know, say that by figuring what the pitcher is trying to deliver they're able to set themselves for it and hit better because of it; and this would be an excellent principle if every batter could always outguess the pitcher. I remember one game in which our team outfigured a pitcher by always swinging at the first ball he pitched; that was because we knew that invariably he made the first ball good. But that's different from guessing right on every ball.

The trouble with "guess hitting" is that it's so frequently misleading. Suppose you've figured that the pitcher is going to deliver a low curve, and you set yourself for it. Then you find a fast ball speeding toward the plate chest high. You haven't time to reset yourself and take a full cut at the ball; the result is either that it sails over for a called strike, or that you whiff at it, or send it off for a foul or easy out.

If, on that same ball, you'd been ready for *any* good pitch, within the strike zone, instead of being prepared only for the one kind of ball (the kind that didn't come), you'd have had a much better chance of hitting it squarely. As a rule, guess hitters have a batting average of around .240. That's why I say "wait for the good ones!"

There's a lot of value to a player in having a bat that fits him—one that has the right weight and length and grip for him. It isn't just individual whim that leads almost every big league player to have his own favorite bludgeon. It's a knowledge, born of long experience, that the bat that is just right has a lot more base hits in it than the one which seems a little too heavy, or too short. Sometimes players use the same bats; more often each one has his own, and guards it jealously. Of course, bats get broken—and there's a lot of wailing around our club houses between the time one of the players breaks a choice weapon and the day (it may be weeks later) that he finds another that suits him as well!

Around some clubs I've known there's a lot of wailing on another score—it comes when a man fails to run out a hit, and it's caused by a manager's bearing down on the batter. Running out every kind of hit is mighty important. It doesn't make any difference if the hit is the simplest kind of grounder to second baseman, if first baseman is all set to field the throw and you're still forty feet from the bag. A thousand things can happen to prevent the completion of the play; and if you're tearing for first you can get there in time to take advantage of every mistake. A fielder can drop a ball and pick it up again in just an instant —but if you're on the ground that instant is long enough to make a great big difference. That's why, on some big league teams, men are fined if they don't run out every hit for all they're worth.

About everything I've told you so far has been connected with the mechanics of hitting. There are some important elements that aren't mechanical. The ones I want to tell you of are these— confidence and determination.

In the most dramatic moment of the great 1925 World's Series young Hazen Cuyler came to bat with what seemed to be the burden of winning or losing the championship on his shoulders. Cuyler was Pittsburgh's right fielder, and known as a fine hitter, but he was facing Walter Johnson, great Washington star, and Johnson had been giving Cuyler serious trouble right along.

There were three men on base, two were out. Washington and Pittsburgh were tied up—each had three games and seven runs in the final game. Cuyler had two strikes and no balls; apparently the great Johnson was to end Pittsburgh's only chance since the Series had opened to take the lead.

Cool as a young Eskimo, Cuyler stood in his box and let two balls whiz past into the catcher's glove. Two and two! When the next ball came Cuyler swung—and the series was all over, for he sent the ball into the field stands, and two men scored. Pittsburgh won the game 9—7 and the championship, four games to three.

Cuyler had confidence and determination. He was confident that he could hit the ball; he did not let the gravity of the situation worry him. He knew his own ability, and refused to give up his belief in it. Moreover, he was determined to do his best. He didn't admit, even to himself, that there was a chance of his failing.

Every batter must have that confidence, and that determination. He has to perfect himself mechanically, of course. He must swing well, watch the ball, pick out the good ones. But he must also have the proper mental attitude toward his work.

If he'll keep all those things in mind, he'll be sure to see his batting average mount.

CHAPTER II

THE WORK OF A PITCHER

BY

ADOLFO LUQUE

PITCHER

ONE day early in the 1926 National League campaign Dazzy Vance, big speedball pitcher for the Brooklyn Robins, turned in a splendid nine innings against our Cincinnati club. It was an important game, because if we lost and Pittsburgh, playing in another city, won, the league leadership went from us to the Pirates. Brooklyn, well up in the race, was eager to take the game.

And Vance pitched masterfully. He fanned fourteen batters, almost tying the National League record of fifteen in nine innings. In the ninth, however, the score was tied up, and Vance was removed for a pinch hitter. Then another pitcher took his place, and when Brooklyn won in the next inning the new pitcher got official credit for the victory—that's a trick of box scoring that gives credit to the man actually working when the game is won, unless his team happens to have been ahead when he enters the game.

THE WORK OF A PITCHER

It was hard luck for Vance, for he deserved real reward for his work. The next day, in the club rooms, a friend was talking to him.

"Too bad it worked out that way," the friend remarked. "What were you trying to do—make a new strike-out record?"

Vance grinned. "No, sir! All I was trying to do was win a ball game!"

It's that kind of baseball—real hard work, with no thought of spectacular stunts but merely the idea of playing most effectively—that makes the good pitcher. Just the same, I want to caution every boy against allowing himself to overwork. If you follow the newspaper accounts of ball games, you'll notice that big league pitchers go on the mound only once every four or perhaps five days. "Iron Man" Joe McGinnity was an exception—he used to pitch two games in an afternoon and sometimes another the next day, and he continued playing until he was more than fifty years old. But not one man in ten thousand has his strength. As a rule, a pitcher does his pitching in comparatively small doses.

Pitchers aren't particularly favored individuals —don't get that idea. The reason for their light work is that it's so much harder on a throwing arm to serve up from three to ten or even twenty balls an inning for nine innings, all of them with considerable speed or jump, than it is to play one of the other positions calling for less throwing.

SECRETS OF BASEBALL

It's been my experience that boys learning to pitch are inclined to forget the necessity for taking care of their arms. They're very unwise, because the youthful pitcher who "burns out" his throwing arm may never get back full strength. I've always played ball—as a boy in Cuba I learned the game, and I kept at it until I landed in the big leagues. But when I was young, fortunately, I didn't overwork myself.

On the other hand, I knew a fellow who, as a young pitcher, seemed destined to be a world-beater. He had unusual speed for a boy, and he worked on control and curves until he had them developed splendidly. His neighborhood team, with him on the mound, won city championships repeatedly; he made a remarkable high school record.

But when he started to play with his college team, as he grew older, he found that he didn't seem to "have the stuff" of his earlier years. He couldn't burn the ball to the catcher for more than an inning or two at a time; his curves didn't break sharply any more; sometimes his control left him completely. "Ed's throwing 'em over the grandstand to-day," was a frequently heard comment.

That player had used his young, growing arm too hard. He had strained it beyond its capacity, so that, just at the time when it should have served him best, it proved to be useless.

THE WORK OF A PITCHER

One more preliminary caution I'd like to give every boy, too—be sure that pitching is the thing you can do best before you try to make a twirler out of yourself. Younger boys, first starting to play baseball, all want to pitch; and sometimes, whether they're good pitchers or not, they carry the desire with them as they become older.

But there's a lot more glory in being a good baseman or outfielder than a bad pitcher—don't forget that. If you don't seem to have special capabilities that make you pitch a good deal better than average, you'll be wise to find some other position to play. . . . Often mighty good pitchers have taken to playing elsewhere in order to be of most value to their teams. Babe Ruth, extremely successful with the Boston Braves as a twirler, became an outfielder so that his batting ability could be brought into every game; and he proved to be not only a great hitter but also a great outfielder. George Sisler, infielder of the St. Louis Browns, was the best pitcher the University of Michigan ever had, and he went to the big leagues as a pitcher. But he found he would be of more value as a first baseman, and he developed into one of the greatest of all time, as every fan knows.

Now, supposing you're convinced that pitching is your forte, how are you going to go about learning the game? The first thing is right in line with what I've said about overwork.

SECRETS OF BASEBALL

Start slowly.

Perhaps you've noticed that major league pitchers and catchers are the first members of the teams to go into spring training each year. That's because it takes so much longer for them to work up to top speed than it does the other players. They start training in February, and it isn't until April that they're ready for full-time work.

Boys can well follow the same schedule. Start lobbing the ball around, perhaps only for a few minutes a day, late in the winter—outdoors if it's warm enough, in a gymnasium or even back in the old barn if the weather stays cold. Don't do anything the first day but play catch for a short while. Extend the time a little the second day, but don't try to throw hard. Keep it up at this pace for a week or two, and lay off entirely for a day or more if you find your arm unusually stiff or sore or tired.

And every time you throw a ball, try to make your movements rhythmical. That, you'll find, is the secret of successful pitching, just as it's the secret of batting, of golf, of rowing, of every kind of active sport. A ball must be propelled by a smooth, thoroughly coördinated movement of body and arm and leg that applies to it, at just the proper moment, all of the effective strength the thrower has.

You'll see what I mean when you watch a good pitcher work. Walter Johnson is the classical example of rhythm, of easy smoothness, of perfect timing. When he first came from the Pacific coast to the big leagues the old players shook their heads.

"Such speed can't last," they predicted. "He's going to wear himself out."

But they didn't count on the fact that he never jerked, never strained to apply terrific force to the ball. Instead, he made each pitch one balanced, coördinated motion. He took advantage of the shift of weight from right foot to left; he threw the ball at just the right moment to get the greatest force behind it; he moved always rhythmically and evenly. That explains his years with the Washington team, and his continued effectiveness.

And that is what boys should work for in the early days of their training, when they're still lobbing balls around and taking things easily. If they get the fundamentals of timing and rhythm in those days, they'll keep them as work gets more strenuous.

During this early practice, keep control in mind. Control is just about the most important single element in effective pitching, and to get it right requires weeks and months of hard work. Practice at making the ball hit exactly where the other fellow is holding his glove; throw at a mark on a fence or wall, if necessary. Remember that you must learn to throw every ball through that "strike zone"—the rectangle with the batter's shoulders and knees as its top and bottom and the home plate's edges as its sides— or just at its corners and borders. I've known boys who made a wooden frame of just the size of a typical "strike zone" and then practiced pitching through it.

All this time, remember, you're taking the work easily. As the weather warms up, however, and as your arm gets accustomed to exercise, you can safely dig in a little harder. Still keeping control and rhythm in mind, throw with a little more speed. Zip the ball in a few times a day so that you hear the satisfying "thunk!" in the catcher's glove. Find out, as you go along, just which speeds seem best for you. And learn to cut the corners of the "strike zone"—to put the ball high or low, inside or outside, as the situation may demand.

It's about at this stage of the game that a good many boys get to thinking about throwing curves. They get impatient for faster progress, and feel that they're not developing rapidly enough into Walter Johnsons and Grover Alexanders; and they dig up out of a back corner of their minds what they've heard about in-curves and out-shoots and hops and breaks. So they make the mistake of working hard on curve balls.

I say "mistake" because, as often as not, it's ill-advised practice of this kind that damages a boy's pitching arm irreparably. It takes a good deal more strength to put a break on a ball than it does to throw a straight ball. It requires a snap and jerk that only a lot of exertion can give. And so it's bad business for a young pitcher to let himself be bothered by what he hears about curves. Sometimes one variety of curve—usually an "out" (that is, one that breaks to the catcher's right)—is naturally easy for a boy to throw, and it's permissible for him to work on that to a limited extent.

But no pitcher can become a Walter Johnson or an Alexander and last as those men have done if, by working on curves, he "throws his arm away" while he's young.

Whatever kind of ball a pitcher is going to throw, however, he should remember this:

Hold the ball the same way *for every pitch.*

To a lot of boys that will seem a pretty harsh rule. Dozens have asked me how I hold an up-shoot and an out-drop and a fast one and a slow ball, and a lot of other kinds of which I've never even made the acquaintance, and my answer is always the same:

"I hold them all alike."

If you're worrying about when to use a "knuckle ball" and when to put your little finger on the northeast corner, when to grip the seam in a particular manner and when not to, you're wasting time. What you must do is find a grip for the ball that, with just the tiniest variations, will enable you to throw every kind of ball you're going to use. The experience of a fellow who came to the big leagues not long ago for a tryout will tell you why.

This man, a tall, rangy chap, had been playing in a Southern mountain town, and a scout had decided that he had a good deal of ability. His fast ball zipped like a bullet, and his curves had real breaks. In his district he was considered a wizard—batters simply couldn't touch him.

So he came to a big league camp for a trial, and after the usual period of preliminary practice was put in a training game. He seemed to have everything on the ball the scout had reported; for an inning or two he breezed along in fine style. Then batters began to find him, and by the fourth they were whaling his offerings all over the lot. At the end of the inning the first baseman on the team, a wise old-timer, solved the difficulty.

"That fellow announces just what kind of ball he's going to throw by the way he grips it," the first baseman said. "No wonder they're getting on to him!"

Of course, the batter can't see how a pitcher is holding the ball; but nine times out of ten the coachers at first and third bases can, and it's simple for them to signal to the batter. That was what had happened in this case. And the

24

habit of changing grips was so strongly ingrained in the pitcher that he had to go back to the mountains to teach himself to standardize—he couldn't work in fast company otherwise.

All the pitchers on the Cincinnati club, and most pitchers on other clubs, use this one-grip system. Grips vary widely, naturally, just as methods of delivery and wind-up and throwing vary; the important thing is for the young pitcher to learn, early, just which grip suits him best, and then to standardize on it.

He must develop, too, a wind-up that isn't so slow as to make stealing easy, or a big lead-off from the base safe for a runner. Pitchers with lengthy, time-taking wind-ups soon get a reputation in the big leagues—every player knows about the weakness—and that is just as true in high school baseball. The fraction of a second that's saved by rapid wind-up is frequently the difference between an out and a man safe on the bag.

That's true not only in the case of a pitched ball followed by a throw by the catcher to a bag, but also when a pitcher is trying to catch a man off first himself. It's up to him to watch that man every minute, and to let the first baseman know he's going to throw; then he has to get the throw off in a flash, and often from an awkward position, for he gives his plan away if he doesn't face the batter as usual, no matter what his intention.

I've found that the best throw to base is the direct overhand peg. Sometimes you see pitchers trying a side-arm or underhand throw; you rarely see it succeed. It isn't as fast a throw as the overhand, and so it shouldn't be used for that purpose. . . . Young pitchers don't always remember, when they're playing in scrub games without an umpire, that every motion to make a throw must be completed. Otherwise such a motion is a balk, and it's heavily penalized. So pitchers shouldn't let themselves get the habit of balking, even in practice. Bad habits like that may crop up at unexpected times, and when they do they are usually disastrous.

One more thing about this matter of overwork in pitching. To my mind, it's just as important to take things easily when it's possible during a game as it is during the early training season. Here's what I mean:

Suppose you're pitching against a team of ordinary strength, some of its batters strong and others weak. Likely you will know ahead of time which of them are most dangerous; if you don't, you can tell by the way they handle themselves at the plate, by what they do their first turns at bat, by their position in the batting order (usually the strongest batters come about third, fourth and fifth in the list—fourth place is called the "clean-up position"). As soon as you know the batters, you can suit your offerings to their abilities. On the dangerous men you can bear down, pitching just as carefully and skillfully as you know how. On the weaker batters you can work a little more easily, conserving your strength for the others.

You'll want to work a good deal harder, too, when there are two men on base and no outs, for instance, than when there is nobody on. You'll put more energy and thought into your pitching when the game is close and your team is only a run ahead, or perhaps just behind, than when you have a big lead. In other words, you'll use your strength when you need it and conserve it when your position is safe.

I advise this because I believe that, in the long run, it pays. It isn't slacking, of course. A horse throws more muscle into the collar when he's going up hill than when he's on the level; but he pulls all the time, regardless. A pitcher uses more skill in danger than in safety. . . . Some mighty successful pitchers—Dazzy Vance is one of them—do not follow this rule closely. Vance works hard every minute he is on the mound, putting his blinding speed on almost every ball. Most of the twirlers to whom I've talked, however, think that this wears down a pitcher unnecessarily soon, and that he'll last longer—and be of correspondingly greater value—if he works the other way.

This business of headwork—of pitching according to the situation—doesn't stop here.

You've hardly begun when you've learned this one lesson.

Suppose the man who is facing you in the seventh inning of a game has made two hits when he's come up to bat before. You think back to those times, and you remember that both times, we'll say, he found a straight ball, waist high and outside the plate, just what he wanted. The conclusion is obvious—if he's given another like those two he's likely to convert it into a third safe hit.

Probably your catcher, who studies batters as closely as you do, has noticed the same thing, and he'll be signalling for some other kind of ball if he has. In any case, your job is to learn batters' strengths and weaknesses, and then use your knowledge to your advantage.

That's where control is invaluable. You must be able to keep the ball low for batters who like to hit high ones, inside for those who are dangerous on outside ones. You must study every batter, too—know just what to give him in order to get, from your point of view, the best results.

Likely you'll find, in the baseball you play, just the thing we find in big league ball—that there are some batters that don't seem to have any weak spots. One day a couple of years ago an American League pitcher had fanned Babe Ruth three times in succession on a particular kind of curve.

He was mightily pleased. "I've found the Bambino's soft point," he gloated.

The next time he came to bat Ruth cracked exactly the same kind of ball for a home run!

Fortunately there aren't many like Ruth and Speaker and Heilmann and Hornsby, however, who seem to take to everything you give them. Most batters have vulnerable spots, and it's up to you to find them.

One thing that a great many boys seem to forget in their pitching is that they have eight men to help them in retiring the batters. It's as much a credit to a pitcher to force the man at the plate to knock a high fly to a fielder, or to roll an easy grounder to a baseman, as it is to strike him out. That's a thing he can learn to do, too, by studying batters' peculiarities and taking advantage of them. Don't try to play the whole game with your pitching arm—your infielders and outfielders are put there to take most of the burden from you.

A good deal of fielding, of course, falls to the lot of the pitcher in a game. Don't neglect that in your practice. Have batters knock rollers and bunts your way, and accustom yourself to handling them easily and smoothly. There's an art to taking a slow-rolling bunt or a fast bounder and shooting it across the diamond to the first baseman without losing an instant of time. You can't afford to lose that instant, either, for it may mean that the runner will be safe if you do.

So get in a lot of practice on things of that kind. Learn to throw almost in the same motion with which you catch or pick up the ball. You'll want to be sure you won't be in the boat with pitchers I've seen, who, unable to field bunts properly, had to be taken from a game because batters attacked their weakness.

After all, good pitching is nothing more than hard, conscientious, intelligent work. As Dazzy Vance said after that splendid game he pitched against the Reds, the aim of a pitcher isn't to make records—it's to win ball games. And he'll win a lot more, and pitch longer, if he goes at it in the right way. Besides, he'll get a lot of fun out of it; for pitching is the kind of work that is the finest sort of play.

CHAPTER III

THE MAN BEHIND THE PLATE

BY

CHARLES L. HARTNETT

CATCHER

IF the average boy catcher—often the pretty good catcher of a pretty good high school team—should suddenly find himself a battery mate for Grover Alexander, formerly of the Chicago Cubs, or for Luque, or the famous Dazzy Vance of Brooklyn, the first ball he'd receive would bring him about the biggest shock of his life.

I mean that literally. It's bound to be a shock to stop a ball that's traveling somewhere in the neighborhood of a mile a minute (scientific tests have proved that Walter Johnson throws a ball at the rate of 120 feet a second, for instance; you can see yourself how fast a ball thrown by an even less speedy pitcher would go). Big league catchers, and the young catchers who have learned their business, know what to do to counteract the shock; but lots of fellows don't. I'll tell you what I mean.

One spring when the Cubs were doing their preseason training out on the Pacific coast a young catcher came to the grounds where we were practicing and, in one way and another, got to throwing the ball around with the rest of us. He was a well-built, sturdy chap, and seemed to know something about catching—he'd played in high school and later with his home town semi-pro team. He threw well, and handled himself well in "playing catch."

It wasn't long, though, until he found himself trying to catch one of our pitchers. At first, while the pitcher was warming up, it went all right. But as the pitcher's speed increased the catcher got into more and more trouble—seemed to be having difficulty keeping his balance after he caught a ball. He'd stagger, and step backward, and look around as though he didn't know what had hit him.

It wasn't the unusual speed he was facing, or the fact that he was playing with big leaguers. It was simply that he didn't do an important part of his job correctly. He didn't set himself firmly to catch the ball.

Setting himself is one of the most important features of a catcher's work, and about the first thing a fellow ought to learn. It means, chiefly, getting the feet placed and braced to meet the rush of the ball. Feet should be spread, with toes pointing slightly out; the body should face squarely to the front. There seems to be an added firmness, a kind of resilience, too, in a slight bending of the knees. It's easy to see that a man can take a shock better if his knees are bent than if he's standing on straight, rigid legs. You'll never see a boxer standing stiff-legged.

Once a fellow has learned to set himself for that thump of the ball, he has a second basic principle to keep in mind. That's called "centering the ball." It means that you should catch the ball squarely in front of the center of your body. Not out at the side, not in your gloved hand alone; exactly in front of you, and with both hands.

"I don't need to be told that," some young catchers have said. "Anybody would know enough to do it that way."

And yet it's surprising how many inexperienced players try time after time to do it the wrong way. Whether it's lack of knowledge or a desire to grandstand a bit, it's a thing that's frequently done. And the fellows who do it don't often become more than second string catchers until they've learned to change their style.

Of course, there are dozens of times when it's utterly impossible to catch a ball just where you want it. Sometimes the pitch is wild, and you have to go up into the air, or stoop low, or jump to right or left; but those times are the exceptions to the rule. Whenever you can, you ought to receive the ball just as squarely in front of you as it's humanly possible.

Ordinarily, his size helps a catcher to hold a hard-pitched ball. There are a few small catchers, like Ray Schalk of the Chicago White Sox, and Washington's "Muddy" Ruel; but most men who play behind the plate are tall, strongly built fellows. Even Schalk and Ruel are exceptionally sturdy.

Lots of young catchers ask me how to judge a curve ball—how I set myself for a sudden last-minute swerve in the ball's path. That's not such a problem as it sounds. For one thing, the "break" in a curve ball is always out in front of the plate, so that the catcher has plenty of time to see the path it's going to take. For another, he knows exactly where the pitcher plans on sending the ball, before it ever starts on its course. So it's a comparatively easy thing to get set for it. There may be a last-instant movement of the hands to meet the ball squarely, but that isn't a thing you stop and think about; it's automatic, and you can't help doing it properly if you've practiced at all.

You've probably noticed that catchers, just before they set themselves to receive the ball, invariably squat on their haunches, hands between their legs. It doesn't take a lot of baseball knowledge to realize that usually they're giving their signals to the pitcher and to the rest of the players when they do that. The pitcher and perhaps the second baseman are about the only ones who can see the catcher's hands in that position. The second baseman will ordinarily pass the signal on to the other players. That squat is a kind of super-bend of the knees, with body upright and perfectly balanced. I've seen catchers who learned to set themselves so well in this position that they were able, with their bent legs and widely spread feet, to receive low balls from the pitcher and to throw back to him without rising.

Big league catchers' ability to keep base stealing a mighty dangerous procedure seems an unattainable thing for lots of young catchers. It shouldn't be. I remember a boy friend of mine who was developing himself into a pretty fair catcher, but who seemed to have a lot of trouble catching stealers at second.

"Trouble is, they're always there when the ball gets down to the bag," he told me ruefully. "I throw just as fast as I can, but they seem to beat me every time. Guess I'm just not cut out to make my high school letter this year."

I knew how much that letter meant to the boy, and he seemed to be getting along fairly well in other ways. So I took the first opportunity I had to watch him play, and here's what I found:

He was throwing with a wide side-arm swing that lost him energy and accuracy on every peg.

His throws were high "rainbows" that seemed

to take forever to get where they were going.

He had a bad habit of aiming for the base-man, rather than for the base.

Well, I pointed out those difficulties in his style of play, and told him how to correct them. I showed him how to throw from right beside his ear, with a fast direct-forward thrust that got the ball off in a hurry, just on the proper line and with more zip to it than he'd ever been able to put into his side-arm swing. I taught him to peg just above the pitcher's head (if he'd been older and stronger, with a harder throw, I'd have made it straight at the pitcher's head), because that's just the height a ball ought to reach at the top of its arc across the diamond. You don't need to be told that the flatter the trajectory of the throw, the more rapidly the ball will get where you want it to go.

And I told the boy to throw, every time, right at the bag and nothing else.

"It's up to the second baseman, or the short-stop, to cover the bag and get the throw," I said. "Your job is to get the ball to the bag. If the baseman's onto his job, he'll be there ahead of time; in any case, you don't need to worry about him. Throw straight for the base—and keep the ball low. If the baseman has to touch the runner out, he'll lose valuable fractions of a second stooping from a high catch."

Those tips seemed to be what the boy needed,

for he made his letter that spring, and the last time I saw him play he looked like a comer. Lots of boys have faults in throwing to second that are similar to his; if they ever expect to get to the stage where they can catch base-running flashes like Max Carey of Pittsburgh, and Kiki Cuyler of the same club, and Frankie Frisch of the New York Giants, they'll have to remember every one of them.

One of the greatest pegs to second in big league history was an interesting freak. Jimmy Archer, catcher with the Cubs some years ago, had fallen into a tanner's vat when he was young, and the boiling tanning fluid constricted the muscles on his throwing arm so that he wasn't able to swing powerfully from overhead—couldn't use the beside-the-head peg such as I described at all. So Archer had to work up an underhand throw, one that flashed out from beside his body. He developed this throw so perfectly that while he was in the big leagues it was the fastest catcher's peg in the game, and one that kept runners well glued to first.

That's no argument for developing a freak throw. It is an argument, though, for working on a weakness until you've beaten it. The fellows who are the best baseball players, on sand lots or in the big leagues, are usually the ones who spend the most time practicing and overcoming faults in their play.

Remember, when you're developing your throw, that you'll frequently have to peg to first or third. The rules are pretty much the same—throw fast in a straight over-shoulder motion, and throw for the bag. Because the distance is so much less, you'll be able to throw a little lower. A smashing shot from catcher to first has caught more than one runner napping, and every backstop ought to try to make his throws down the line as effective as he possibly can. One of "Muddy" Ruel's big assets is his ability to keep runners chained to the bag.

That throw comes in mighty well at another time—when you're fielding a bunt. This particular play is an art all by itself—if you've ever seen old-time catchers like Johnny Kling, and Wally Schang, or younger players such as Cochrane of the Athletics, you'll realize that there's more to it than just picking up a ball.

In the first place, a catcher has to be on his toes every instant. Of course, he can usually tell a fraction of a second ahead of the crack of the bat whether the hitter wants to bunt; either the situation on the diamond or the attitude of the batter tells him that. But he must always be ready to jump like a shot to recover a ball in home plate territory; and he has to move particularly fast because the ball will be moving away from him—not toward him, as it always does in relation to every other player on the team.

38

In the second place, he has to remember that he can't waste any time, after he recovers the ball, in whirling and getting set for the throw. For instance, if the bunt is a short one down the third base line, he can't go tearing into the diamond and field the ball with his back toward the first base line. If he did, the runner, nine times out of ten, would get to the bag far ahead of his throw for the simple reason that he'd have to shift before he could make the peg.

Every time, therefore, he must do what we call "keeping the ball in front of him." He must go after it, so that, when he gets his hand on it, he'll be in near-to-perfect throwing position. That means facing first if the proper play is a throw to first; facing second if there's a good chance of a force play there (though such a play on a bunt is rare); facing third if that's where the situation calls for him to throw. It seems like a pretty stiff order, this "keeping the ball in front." But it won't be if you practice every chance you get and keep the rule in mind all the time.

Practice means a whole lot to a catcher. Probably you've seen professional teams practice before a game—a man at the plate knocking grounders to all the infielders and bunts to the catcher every time his turn comes around. That isn't nearly enough practice. He ought to get some fellow to knock bunts for him to field by the hour.

And the backstop who doesn't want to have everybody laughing at him has to put in a lot of work on another feature of the game, too. That's catching foul tips. It seems easy enough to the fellow sitting in the grand stand; but there aren't many things so deceiving as those high foul flies. They go a long way up in the air, and when they come down they're traveling fast; moreover they don't seem to come just where you expect them, sometimes. So ask that fellow who's helping you to learn to field bunts to vary it with some foul tips now and then.

One thing I haven't told you about is covering the plate properly when a runner is coming in.

When I was a boy playing with scrub and pick-up teams I always was troubled by fellows coming in to score at the plate—it seemed to me that sometimes they managed to get in safe when I should have put them out. I used to plant myself with one foot on the plate (or the shingle or flat rock or whatever we happened to be using) and the other way out at the side, and the runners simply slid in while I was trying to get the ball down to meet them.

As I grew older and went into better baseball, I realized that I'd been leaving the door wide open for them. I should have been standing squarely in their path, instead of off to the side;

then I'd have been able to prevent their coming directly into the plate. Blocking them off is a trick every catcher should have in his bag.

"What about getting spiked?" some boys have asked me. Well, I never let it worry me. After all, there are few close plays at the plate, and when men do slide in they usually come into the side of my shoe. So there's no spiking to it. Injuries of this kind are few and far between, and the less a chap thinks about them the less chance he has of experiencing them.

Another thing you'll see good catchers do is run down the base line to back up plays at first and third—particularly first. Wally Schang used to be down there behind first base right along with the runner, always ready to back up Wally Pipp, or Lou Gehrig, the Yankees' first basemen, if they should happen to miss the ball. That's a mighty good move for a catcher to make. Keep it in mind, in practice and in games.

Just about everything I've told you so far has to do with the mechanical part of a catcher's work—how to throw, how to catch a ball, how to field. There's another side to the part a catcher must play in a ball game, though—a side that is of tremendous importance.

That's what the fans call "using his bean."

For one thing, the catcher has to know just about everything there is to know about the batters on opposing teams. The pitcher with whom he's working will know a lot about them, of course; but usually the catcher knows more, and since it's up to him to give most of the signals, to "work" the batter and to decide what kind of pitch will do the most good (or harm, as far as the batter's average is concerned), he has to study each batter carefully.

Here's what I mean. One season a young outfielder joined one of the teams in the National League, and for a time he seemed to be hitting wild. He had built up a pretty good reputation by the time Chicago played its first game with his team, and in that game he kept up his reputation —made three hits. But—

In that first game I noticed that, surprisingly, the balls he hit were usually inside balls, close to his body and fairly high. So I determined to try him the next day on low balls outside. I signaled the pitcher every time he came up for that kind of ball, with a few variations to keep him guessing, and he didn't do a thing. It wasn't long before other catchers had discovered that he had weaknesses, and his average slumped a lot.

That's what a catcher has to look for. He must have tucked back in his mind a catalogue of every batter's likes and dislikes, so that he can help the pitcher to work against him to best advantage. He has to learn batters' individual habits, too. One dangerous hitter always warned me that he was planning to bunt, I remember, by changing the position of his feet in the box. Another invariably looked away from the pitcher and toward the runner on base when he was going to try to hit the next one. A third who thought he could outguess the battery always seemed to relax his grip on the bat when he figured a wide one was coming, so I could always signal for a fast one over the plate and get a called strike on him.

There are plenty of things like that a catcher must always have in mind. He must keep an eye on men on the bases all the time, too; he must signal to the first sacker when he thinks there's a chance of catching a runner off first, and throw like a flash when the time comes. He must picture every situation keenly, and figure out ahead of time what the proper play is going to be.

Then, too, a catcher must be a kind of anchor to windward for a ball team. Lots of times you've seen a catcher nonchalantly saunter out toward the pitcher and hand him the ball—that isn't just a grand stand move, but usually a step taken to calm down or reassure a twirler who is becoming a bit excited. An unruffled catcher, one who won't let himself get rattled, means a lot to a team. Johnny Bassler of Ty Cobb's Detroit Tigers was considered the most valuable man on his team for several years, largely because he was so successful in keeping pitchers from going up in the air, and in developing confidence in young moundsmen.

Just a word about equipment. I've seen boys catching behind the plate without any apparatus except a glove and a mask. That's bad business. There's no telling when a foul tip or a fast-breaking ball is going to elude the glove and crash into ribs or knee-cap, cause a charley-horse or bruise a bone, if you're not properly protected. And protection means not only a good mask but also shin guards, with big leather knee pads, and a chest protector that will actually protect. Believe me, it's mighty comforting to hear the hollow "plunk!" of a ball socking into that big pad and to realize that it might have been you it hit!

It's important to pick out the right glove, too, and to break it in and become thoroughly accustomed to it. Ira Thomas, who was a star catcher with the Philadelphia Athletics in their World's Championship days around 1910, was a stickler for having the right glove—all major league catchers are, for that matter. But I'd like to pass on to young catchers the advice Thomas gave to Jack Finn, catcher on the Williams College team when Thomas was coach:

"Get yourself a good glove. Break it in slowly—maybe you won't want to use it for more than a few minutes each day for the first several weeks. Then, when it fits your hand perfectly, and you're used to it, don't use any other."

THE MAN BEHIND THE PLATE

A good glove will last a boy a long time, and it's good sense to get the best your pocket will permit. Naturally any glove will wear out in time, and that means picking out and breaking in another.

Being a catcher isn't easy—there are a lot of knocks and hard work to the job. But it's a position on the ball team that's mighty important, and the fellow who has the strength and special ability will get a lot of fun out of it. Moreover, he can improve himself right along if he wants to—he can learn to handle himself properly both mechanically and mentally. And that's where the "kick" in baseball comes—in the pleasure of becoming a regular rather than a scrub player.

CHAPTER IV

THE JOB OF PLAYING FIRST

BY

HENRY LOUIS ("LOU") GEHRIG

FIRST BASEMAN

'WONDER whether I'd make a good first baseman?" a high school athlete asked me once. I replied with a question that made him think, at first, I was "razzing" him.

"Can you catch a baseball?" I said. Then I explained what I meant. Was he a sure catch? Did he have confidence in his own ability to hold onto every throw that came within reaching distance? Did he feel certain, in other words, that he'd be able to stop every ball that came to him? Those were the things I wanted to know.

"Of course a first baseman has to catch balls," was this fellow's answer, "but so does every other player. Why should a first baseman be more certain than anybody else?"

Well, he shouldn't, necessarily. But here's the point—a first baseman who misses throws is going to cause a lot more trouble to his team than a second baseman, or a shortstop, or an outfielder. The reason is that so many more throws are made to the first baseman than to anybody else on the team. If you're familiar with box scores, you know that frequently the first sacker makes more than a third of the putouts for his team. The answer, of course, is that balls were thrown to him—and that he held onto them.

That's why I want a young first baseman, first of all, to realize the importance of being a "sure catch."

There are plenty of things to know, of course, about proper handling of a ball. One of the first things a fellow should work on is form on ground balls. Development of the right kind of form takes time—I advise every infielder to put from three to five weeks on it. Some players get it down pretty well in less than that, but extra practice doesn't hurt anybody.

The easiest rule to remember in fielding ground balls is this: cut out all extra motion. Your aim is to get hold of the ball. The fastest way you can do it well is the best form, and every extra twist of arm or leg or body means a lost instant. So learn to eliminate waste movements.

Remember always to keep your eye on the ball. That can't be overstressed. From the moment the bat starts it on its way until it socks into your mitt, don't take your eye off it. You'll avoid a lot of muffs and fumbles if you follow this rule. Your ideal fielding position is one with knees bent slightly forward and outward, body bent forward just a little at the hips. You'll be resting the brunt of your weight on the balls of your feet.

Learn from the start to get your body in front of the ball whenever possible. Sometimes, of course, you can't do it—you'll be tearing at top speed and will be lucky to get near it. When you can, though, plant yourself squarely in its path. Then, if you misjudge a hop of the ball, or it makes a freak bound, it's likely to hit your body and fall dead, and you can still make a play. It's just as important to keep your eye on the ball in such a case as at any other time. Don't waste precious seconds, if the ball drops to the ground, in looking around for the runner; grab the horsehide and field it. You can always look afterward!

In fielding a ball, your hands should form a pocket, with fingers either straight up or straight down. If they're down for a low ball, the two little fingers should touch, or nearly touch; if up for a high one, the two thumbs should be close together. I don't need to warn most players about the foolishness of one-handed catches when two-handed stops are possible. "Circus catches" look fine—unless they go wrong, as they're mighty likely to do.

I've found it a good idea to start fielding practice indoors, on a wooden floor. When I was trying out for the Columbia University team, Coach Andy Coakley used to get his men into the gymnasium for the first week of practice, and we threw grounders to each other before they even put up the batting cage. Coach Coakley's scheme was an excellent one for early spring work, before outdoor ball weather had put the turf in playing condition.

The reason a wooden floor is good, of course, is because the ball is easier to field. It bounds straight and true on the smooth surface, and it's not apt to make the freak hops you'll get in outdoor work. Learning to handle balls indoors, therefore, gives a player confidence in his fielding ability. Later, when he's on turf or grass, conditions won't be so ideal; but he'll have laid an excellent groundwork in his indoor practice.

Just a few general rules for playing grounders:

Always play the ball—don't let it play you.

On a ball hit not too hard, get in front of it and advance as much as possible before it reaches you.

On a very slow hit, cut in on the ball and get to it as soon as possible.

On a hard hit, get there in a hurry. On smashing grounders there's not much time for maneuvering; the thing is to get in their path in the quickest way possible.

One of the things I've learned about handling a very slow-rolling bunt, or a ball that's stopped rolling, is to grasp it from the top. That's faster and gives a better grip. But if the ball is rolling with some speed, or bounding, I cup it from beneath.

Because a bunt is always pretty slow, it makes throwing harder. There isn't time to straighten up from the crouch and get set for a throw, and that means that often you have to peg the ball from just about the position you're in when you get hold of it. Practice on that kind of throw all you can—it'll be worth while. And watch Lu Blue, Detroit Tigers' first baseman, if you have a chance. Blue is a corking good example of the man who can effectually make those crouch throws.

A first baseman doesn't throw as much as other infielders; but that doesn't mean he shouldn't perfect his throwing. He should learn an overhand peg, instead of the side-arm swing that a good many boys use. He should guard against straining his arm, either by too much early-season throwing or by whaling away with it before it's properly warmed up. A fellow should never go into a game unless he's practiced enough beforehand to limber his muscles.

Accuracy and control, together with speed, are the things to work on in throwing. Teach yourself to gauge the position of the fellow who's receiving the ball from you, and to throw right *at* him—not merely in his general direction. Always feel as if the next pitched ball will be hit directly at you. While the pitcher is winding up, size up the situation and make up your mind what you will do with the ball when it is hit to you.

Footwork plays a surprisingly big part in the work of a good first baseman. It isn't so surprising, of course, if you think it over. Much of a first baseman's playing is done with one of his feet touching the bag; so he's forced to develop a scheme of footwork which will let him move freely and rapidly, and cover a lot of territory, and still maintain that contact with the bag.

The basis of proper footwork is a position with each heel touching an inside corner of the bag. They shouldn't be *on* the bag, as many boys wrongly think; they should be merely *against* it. From such a position as this it's easy to shift to get balls thrown to one side or the other. You're standing, for instance, right in front of the bag, heels against it, and a ball is thrown over to the left. At once you shift so that your right heel is against the left corner of the bag. That brings your body over to the left, and you can take the throw.

Practice on the shift—work on it every day without bothering about catching throws. You should be able to make the shift to either side lightning-fast, with never a thought about it. Learn to do it exactly right, with assurance and without waste motions.

Boys who have watched such first basemen as George Sisler, or Joe Judge, or Bottomley—any good first basemen, in fact, whether they're with big league teams or not—have noticed that, on a close play, they'll often lean far forward to make a catch. That's a variation of the shift, and a valuable one. A first baseman's aim is usually to catch a ball before the runner toes the bag, so if he can save a precious fraction of a second by stretching out toward the ball he must do it. To make this kind of play, you'll have one toe on the bag, the other leg stretched far out toward the thrower. Arms stretch out, too. It's a pretty kind of catch, and an effective one.

The value of that stretch to a first baseman is usually increased by the fact that he's tall—you'll notice that not many first sackers are little fellows. George Kelly of the New York Giants towers six and a half feet into the air; Earl Sheely, of the White Sox, and Jack Fournier and young Babe Herman, of Brooklyn, are big fellows. I am six feet tall myself. Height helps, so if you're tall you're going to have an advantage at the start.

Here's another tip on position when you're going to receive a throw: crouch just a little, with knees bent slightly. Then, if the throw is low, you're easily able to go down for it. If it's high, you can straighten up just as easily.

On a bunt, where the catcher must field the ball, it is a good idea to put the left foot on first, face toward the catcher at home and extend the right foot on the diamond toward second. The right foot is taken out of the way in this manner, and the first baseman is made a good target for the catcher's throw. This position reduces the danger of the ball's hitting the runner as he comes down the line, too.

You'll probably work out a style of your own for your footwork when there's a man on first. I stand as Sisler does—with right heel on the inside corner of the bag which extends into the diamond, touching the side-wall of the bag; other players like other styles better. I prefer this position because it gives me half the bag and the runner half; if I keep to my half and he to his, there's little danger that I'll be spiked.

The first sacker who, with the pitcher's aid, can catch men napping at the bag is mighty valuable to his team. It's good baseball psychology to put a man out after he's put himself on base, for it tends to take a little of the "fight" out of his team. But it isn't an easy thing to do. Hal Chase, one of the greatest of first basemen, was particularly good at it because of the ease and grace—which meant, in turn, the speed—of movement he developed in tagging a man out. Joe Judge is another excellent example.

To develop this speed, you'll have to practice a lot. It's good business to swing your arm down as though tagging a runner every time you take a throw in practice; that accustoms you to the motions, and makes them easy and natural.

Notice that I said "swing your arm *down*"? I meant by that that you should learn to tag a runner on his legs or feet. Then, whether he comes into the base upright or sliding, you're sure to touch him. You wouldn't be sure if you'd learned to tag him high—half the time you'd be thrown out of balance trying to get low. . . . The ball should be gripped tightly, for runners often try to knock a loosely held ball out of a baseman's hand by the force of their legs and feet if he hasn't a good hold on it.

Catching a man napping is largely a question of well-synchronized motion—of the fastest kind of work by the pitcher, and of perfect harmony between him and the first baseman. There's a lot to gain by long practice with a pitcher, as is shown in actual games. Every now and then you hear of a pitcher and a first baseman who work particularly well together, who make records for catching runners off base. It's almost always because they have worked together to perfect the play, and know each other's motions thoroughly. Timing is a big factor.

One of the things a first baseman must keep in mind every minute is his position when nobody is on base. Know the individual batting habits of the men at the plate—you should study every batter—and play according to his style of hitting.

Suppose you know that the batter is a left field hitter, and that he's slow. You'll play deep and farther from the bag than ordinarily. But if he's fast you must play nearer the bag. It is always a question of being in such position that you can cover a lot of ground and still beat him to the sack.

If the batter ordinarily hits to right field, you'll play pretty close to the bag—deep if he is a slow runner, closer in if he's fast.

Handling bunts and "drags" causes an inexperienced first sacker a good deal of trouble. When they're played properly they'll be among the finest plays he'll make, however. I remember one that occurred in a game in 1925 between the Yankees and the St. Louis Browns.

I had hit a slow hopper right over the inside corner of first base, and George Sisler, playing his regular position, dashed over to field it. He managed to reach it at the edge of the grass, almost on the foul line back of the base. It was not going fast, and Sisler got it low and out of position. Somehow he threw it under his right arm (he is a left-hander) to Giard, the St. Louis pitcher, who had come over to cover the bag, and Giard and the ball arrived there just before I did!

Altogether, it was one of the finest plays I have ever seen. Sisler had no time to set himself, he threw the ball on the run. But he sent it straight and true, and with the excellent coöperation of Giard made an out from what appeared at first to be a sure hit.

"The ordinary first baseman can't make a play like that," a boy objected to me when I was describing it to him. Perhaps he was right. But the young first baseman who does his best to learn to make every play in the right way, to be on the alert, never to be caught off guard, is going to find himself making better and better efforts.

When a bunt is expected, the first baseman should play pretty well in—about at the edge of the grass. If he sees that pitcher or catcher can field a bunt, however, he should try to get back to the base to receive the ball. When he's forced to field it himself, he will count on having first covered by pitcher or second baseman.

Often the play will be too fast for him to complete himself; then he must throw rapidly to the man who is covering the bag. It means an underhand throw in most cases, and often one from an awkward position, as I've told you. Let me say again that every boy who wants to become a real first sacker must work on this kind of throw. Lu Blue and Earl Sheely, as well as Sisler, are particularly adept at it.

Remember that the ball should always reach the man covering the bag a step or two *before* he reaches the bag. Time the throw so that the other player will take it on the run, and will have it when he tags the sack. That speeds up the play and makes it more certain; for the fielder isn't going to have time to stop, look for the bag and then receive the ball!

Boys have asked me often about the best way to play when the bases are full, or when two men are on. That's a question that can only be answered with regard to the particular situation, the particular abilities of the runners and a lot of other special circumstances. A few general rules, however, may help.

With men on first and second, it's often well to play back, in your regular position off the bag. One reason is that the man on first will not try to steal with a man on second. Another is that the man on first may be fooled into taking an extra long lead; if he does, the first baseman will have a chance, after he has signaled to the catcher, or caught the catcher's signal, to get back to the base and, by means of a fast throw from the plate, catch the runner off base.

The danger of this play is that the man on second may take advantage of the opportunity to cut for third. The first baseman, however, if he's on the job, can usually keep his eye on that runner at the other side of the diamond and relay the ball to the third baseman in time to catch him if he tries to go over.

Remember that, as I said, different circumstances will completely alter a first baseman's play in similar cases. If the runner on first is specially fast on the bases, for instance, it's good for the baseman to play close enough to hold him from taking too long a lead. That will give second baseman or shortstop a better chance to complete a double play if the opportunity arises.

Another "special circumstance": suppose there's a man on third, and it's a close game. Then you'll want to play in on the edge of the infield grass so that, if a ball is hit to you, you can field it that much sooner and make a quick relay to the plate to catch the runner there.

And here's another, one that comes up more often in high school and college baseball than in big league games: there are men on first and second, and none out. A bunt is expected. As first baseman you play well in on the grass. Catcher signals for a "waste ball"—a ball thrown too wide of the plate for the batter to hit—and you charge in, to give the runner on first the impression that you expect to field a bunt. Meanwhile second baseman is sneaking over to cover your bag, as the runner (if the ruse works) takes an unusually big lead. Catcher shoots the ball down to first, where second baseman takes the throw. Often, then, he can trap the runner.

I could go on indefinitely outlining those special circumstances and special plays. But you'll find it fun to work them out yourself, and easy, too, after you get started on them. Surprise plays will win a lot of ball games.

I hardly need to say again that practice is the first essential in becoming a good ball player—practice in fielding, catching, throwing; batting, too, but I'm not talking about that department of the game. A good development exercise for fielders is the game I've heard called "runner-up"—it consists of getting a runner on the paths with basemen working to put him out. This demands fast, accurate throwing, sure footwork and quick thinking. You can easily invent half a dozen similar games. Exercises in fielding bunts are excellent.

A fundamental of good baseball play is relaxation—don't let yourself become tense and stiff. Learn to keep on your toes, to watch everything keenly, to play rapidly—but always to be natural in movement and to keep your muscles supple and relaxed. Don't let yourself get excited, either. The ball player who loses his head, who can't keep cool, is worse than no ball player at all.

And finally, remember what I told you right at the start—don't try to play first base if you can't catch, and never, when you're playing, take your eye off the ball!

CHAPTER V

STUDY YOUR OPPONENTS

BY

HAROLD J. ("PIE") TRAYNOR

THIRD BASEMAN

IF you're going to play third base, you've got to train yourself to out-think the fellows you're trying to beat.

Fast thinking—and plenty of it—is the key to playing a good game at third. Of course, every great player, no matter what his position, is a thinker. Roger Peckinpaugh of Washington at short, Frankie Frisch of the New York Giants at second, Catcher Johnny Bassler of the Detroit team—these and scores of others have made their marks largely because they were good thinkers. But in some ways third basing takes more baseball brainwork than other positions. The good third baseman has to be alert mentally every minute, so that he can think and move faster than the other fellow.

That means that he has to know a whole lot about the other fellow. He has to know where a batter is strong, where he's weak; how a base runner slides, how closely he watches the pitcher, how long a lead he takes. He has to watch every move, not only of batter and base runner, but also of his own team—to be ready for any situation and to act like lightning when the time comes.

And he has to work with the other men on his team like part of a well-oiled machine. Here's what I mean:

When Wilbur Cooper, veteran pitcher, was with the Pirates he and I worked together particularly well. One put-out play we put over successfully seven times in two seasons—and that's often, for in big league baseball, where games are frequently won by one run, a put-out at third means a good deal. Here's one case that is typical:

Pittsburgh was playing St. Louis, and in the Cardinals' half of the ninth we were leading, 3--2. Hi Myers hit a double, and Manager Hornsby put Jack Smith, a fast man on the paths, in to run for him. The next batter sacrificed Smith down to third, and he took an average-length lead toward the plate.

Cooper was pitching. I saw him give me the signal that he wanted to catch Smith off the base, so as he started to throw I dove for the bag. True to our practice, the ball came shooting to me right at the knees. I caught Smith off base by a hair, and he was out. The batter hit a single—a clout that would have scored Smith. But we held the man on first, and won.

Three other times that play won games—and all because Cooper and I had worked it to the finest point we knew how. Cooper's signal was one the runner would never notice—that's important. Then his execution was fast and perfect. He threw in a flash, and true as an arrow the ball reached the bag knee high—at the position easiest for me to catch it and make a pass at the runner. Moreover, our practice had enabled me to time myself exactly right—to start for the bag as late as possible, so as not to alarm the runner, and yet to get there in time.

Practice made that play a winner. Practice taught me just what to expect from Cooper, and him to have confidence in me. We learned to work together. And that's what all ball teams must do. . . . Of course, other pitchers and I weren't able to make the play go so well; that's a difference in men. On some plays I was more successful with other pitchers than with Cooper. Your job is to know all the abilities of the men you work with as well as those of your opponents, and then to make the most of your knowledge.

To do this you must be able to play your position almost perfectly, mechanically. One of the most important features of third base play is the position of the baseman.

Ordinarily I play about five steps from the bag —back of it and toward second base. The third baseman can't play as far from the bag as short-

stop and second baseman do, for several reasons
—you'll see what they are as I go along. His
usual position must be such that he can cover
the bag in a flash when necessary, can go in for
grounders or can go back for pop flies.

Every boy knows, though, that one of the most
important jobs a third baseman has is covering
bunts, and that in order to do it the player must
leave his "usual" position often. So I'm going
to talk about bunts and how to play them, first.

It's easy to see why a third baseman gets so
many bunts down his way. Batters—unless
they're Ty Cobbs—don't often bunt to make safe
hits; they bunt so that the runner on first can
advance to second, even at the cost of an out at
first. But even if their own safety at first isn't the
primary thing, there's much more chance of their
making it when the bunt is down the third base
line because of the longer throw. So most bunts
go that way, and the third baseman has to be
on his toes every minute, in order to save every
instant in getting the ball across the diamond.

Let's suppose a runner is on first, and there
is none down. The logical play, then, is a bunt.
Of course, teams don't always bunt in a case like
that, any more than a football team always punts
on the fourth down—if they did, the game would
lose half its thrill. But because it's the regular
play, the third baseman has to set himself for

it if he hasn't some very good reasons to think something else is coming.

All right. I'm watching that man at the plate, to see if he's choking his bat as many men do when they plan to bunt. I take my position five feet inside the base line from third to home, and about the same distance from the second-third base line—in a big league park it's just about on the edge of the grass. That sounds as though it's pretty far over to the right. It's not too far, though. One reason is that so many bunts come slithering down the third base line itself—right toward the bag.

Another is that it's usually a whole lot easier for a fielder to go to his left than to his right. The third baseman's glove is on his left hand (I've never known of a left-handed third baseman, and don't see how a port sider could play the position most effectively), and that seems to enable him to cover more territory to the left than to the right. So it's wise for him to be fairly near the base line.

The ball comes from the batter—when the pitcher delivered it the runner on first scratched for second. I see that it's going to be fair, and that it's a good bunt—not very hard hit, but with enough force so that the catcher can't field it. It's far to the pitcher's right, say. So it's up to me. All this I've noted in an instant, and in that instant I must start straight at the ball.

STUDY YOUR OPPONENTS

That's a thing to remember—don't wait for the ball to come to you. If you do, the runners will be safe all around before you ever touch the horsehide. You've got to go after it and meet it as soon as possible—frequently it will be half-way down to the plate. . . . Watch for the chance of the ball rolling foul. If it goes outside the base line before it gets to the bag, it's foul; and sometimes, when I see it dribbling right along the line with an apparent tendency to roll out, I don't field it at all, but wait until it has actually crossed the line. Then I trap it and hold it until the umpire has had an opportunity to see that it was actually out. Of course, if I'm not pretty certain that it's going out (and you can't always be *sure* of that), it's a foolish play to try to make, for the runner will be safe in a walk. But when it has that tendency to the right, and the situation isn't a dangerous one, it's not a bad thing to keep in mind.

Back to that fair ball, though, with the runner from first almost to second. I know there's not time to make a double play of it; so I grab the ball and set myself at the same time for the throw to first. The throw must be a good one; it must go low and fast, and straight for the bag, if possible. It's important to get it off in a hurry, even at the expense of perfect accuracy, however. Send it any place within two or three feet of the first baseman's position, and it's up to him to stop it. That gives you a good target, at that—it's equivalent to a barn door six feet high and close to six feet wide. So you should be able to hit it.

That's the simplest form of bunt. I wish they were all of that variety. Unfortunately they're not. About the hardest play a third baseman has to make is the bunt with men on both first and second. In that case he has a chance to make a forced out at third; but it's a slim chance, for the runners on the bases will have started almost before the crack of the bat, and unless everything works perfectly all three men are going to be safe.

Again the question of working well with the pitcher becomes important. The pitcher, you see, has to cover the bag on this play; and he must do his part just as expertly as the third baseman. That's partly to give the baseman confidence. I like to know that when I cage the bunted ball and whirl to throw to the bag the pitcher's going to get there in time to receive it. The play really depends on that and one other feature—successful timing of the throw by the fielder. Usually the pitcher won't quite have reached the bag when you're ready to throw; so you must time the ball so it will get to him just exactly as he steps on the sack. Timing the throw for a case like that is a thing that takes plenty of practice.

STUDY YOUR OPPONENTS

There are many other bunt-situations, and each must be met in its own way. The reason Joe Dugan of the New York Yankees was such a good third-bagger was largely that he was ready to work out each play properly as it came up—he thought lightning-fast. I won't try to outline all the possible plays for a third baseman built around a bunt; you'll meet them in games again and again. So spend every instant you can get in practicing on bunt plays. Have the batter, in fielding practice, knock you every kind of bunt; figure on each one just what you would do for a given situation. "One out, a man on second on this bunt," you will say to yourself, for instance. Then by the time you've got the ball in your throwing hand you know just what you're going to do with it.

I told you a while ago that you ought to watch how the batter holds his stick, to see if he perhaps plans on bunting. There are lots of other signs you must watch. His legs may give away his intentions, for some batters stand entirely differently for different kinds of hitting. His eyes may tell you what you want to know—the direction of his glance. I remember one team that informed me plainly every time it intended to try a bunt by the kind of signal it used—a kind of twist the batter gave his cap just before the ball was pitched. Keep on the lookout for little things like a hitch to the breeches, or patting the dust in a particular manner, or that cap-twist—you're likely to get more than one signal by careful watching.

Let's go back to the "ordinary third base play"—the kind in which the fielder is playing in his usual position and not expecting a bunt. I've told you where he'll be—approximately. But don't get the idea that that's a hidebound rule. If you have ever watched any of the big time third basemen—Oswald Bluege, the nervy Washington third sacker, for instance, or Willie Kamm of the Chicago White Sox, or the youngster Fred Lindstrom of the New York Giants—you'll notice that they move a little with every batter. More than that. They move almost with every ball pitched.

The reason is easy to see. Batters have certain individualities in their hitting, and you have to play for them. Cy Williams, slugger with Philadelphia's National League club, always makes his hits to right field; that means that the three fielders and the four men on the base lines must play farther to the right when Williams comes to bat (that actually means farther to their own left) than they would in many other circumstances. Most batters aren't so regular in hitting to one section of the park, but they all have certain propensities that you get to know and play for.

More important, particularly when you don't

know the player, is to watch the ball pitched. I get the signal on every pitch as to what kind it's going to be—Glenn Wright, the shortstop who made such a fine showing in the 1925 World's Series, relays them to me after getting them from the catcher—and I place myself accordingly. If it's to be a fast ball and the hitter is left-handed, I hug the base line pretty close, because he's likely to connect with it just a little late and send it toward left field. If it's a slow ball to a right-hander, I do the same—he'll probably hit it early and send it toward left.

Figure those things out for yourself. They're simple. Then, once you've figured them out, make them help you with your work.

It's just as important to go in fast on a hard-hit grounder as it is to meet a bunted ball. Every instant, every step saved in getting the ball to first means that much more chance of putting the batter out. So dash in to meet balls. Plan on getting them in front of you, too. It's bad business taking balls in one hand or off to the side if there's any way to avoid it. It's fatal if you play to "knock down" hot grounders, as I do. By "knocking down" grounders I mean stopping them with your hands and letting them fall before you, then recovering them in a hurry and throwing them to first, or second, or wherever the play is to be made. It's a style of play I like, but a good many players don't. Bluege, for instance, one of the best third basemen in the American League, doesn't use it at all. He stops balls and holds onto them, throwing them without the "knock down" feature. There's no question that this second method is the faster, and whenever it's a necessity to save every instant I use it. But I find the other style satisfactory when there's a little more time.

Every boy knows that a third baseman must have a good throwing arm. I was moved from shortstop to third when I came to Pittsburgh largely because my peg across the diamond seemed to be unusually strong. I made this mistake—I burned every throw across to Grimm, or McInnis, or Grantham just about as hard as I could throw, and it wasn't long before I found that my arm was weakening a little. So I learned to conserve my strength. It's often necessary to send the ball across like a bullet, and no strength should be spared when there's a hurry. But don't overwork your arm just because it's a good one. An easier throw is just as good, and perhaps surer, when there's time.

That doesn't mean you should waste any seconds. Third basemen must be fast-moving players—if they're not they'll never get to be top notchers. Fritz Maisel of the Baltimore team in the International League was a third baseman with lots of ability, but one great fault that big league managers couldn't overlook. He didn't

get started fast enough. Learn to move just as
rapidly as you possibly can. A fast start helped
me a whole lot in making a World's Series play
in 1925. It was on a hot liner from Sam Rice's bat
in the second game, and everybody said afterward
that it looked like a sure double. But fortunately I'd schooled myself to start fast on a
play, and I managed to get far enough into the
path of the ball to stab it. The play cut off
some Washington runs that might have won the
game for them.

A third baseman, like all the others, must often
go back for pop flies, and he ought to devote
as much time as possible to practicing on them.
Get somebody to hit up high, short fungoes, and
learn to chase back from your base line position
to the field to drag them in. Learn to judge them
accurately, and to catch them safely. There's
mighty little excuse for a dropped fly, if you're
able to get under it.

One fault that I've seen in young players is
inability to move *sidewards* as well as forward
and back. I remember a boy on a high school
team in a little town near Pittsburgh who was a
flash at running in to meet grounders, but who
tumbled all over his feet—awkward as an
ostrich—when balls came to his right or left.
His value to his team was much decreased by
that one fault.

Moreover, he could have improved his play a

lot in that respect, if he'd tried. I've spent hours in what I call spike-shoe practice—it's really a kind of sideward running in regular baseball shoes. Before I came to Pittsburgh I found that I wasn't able to move to the side as rapidly as I wanted to, so I set in to improve. I put on my spikes and dashed from side to side, all by myself—must have looked like a new kind of dancer to any one who didn't know what I was aiming at. Anyway, the result was that I could move faster and keep my balance better. It's an exercise I'd advise every baseman to try.

Another thing that bothers young basemen a lot is tagging a runner. No need for it to do so. Base runners aren't out to spike a baseman, and if he handles himself properly they won't do it. I always try to block the runner off from the base, for instance, and that sounds dangerous; but I rarely get a scratch. I put my foot right in the base line, between the runner and the bag; that means that when he slides for the base he'll be met by my foot instead. My shoe is always scarred for this reason—spikes coming into it. But that kind of spiking doesn't hurt, and it always helps to put the runner out.

In all this I've told you I've taken it for granted that the fellow playing at third, or studying the position, is sure that he's fitted for the job. He's fast; he has a good throwing arm. He uses his head; he has what is known as "a good pair of hands" for fielding. That means big, strong hands—Lutzke of Cleveland had hands par excellence, and was effective for that reason. He practices hard, he takes hints from men who know the game better than he does. He seizes every chance to improve his handling of bunts and speedy grounders, pop flies and sizzling liners.

And, on top of it all, he makes his job a study of human nature. He studies the men he's working against—their peculiarities of style and temperament. And he knows, and relies on, the fellows he's playing with. When Wilbur Cooper gave me the signal for a sudden throw to third, I felt absolute confidence that the throw would come just exactly where it would be most effective, and that Cooper would get the ball to the sack just as I reached the spot. I knew Cooper, and Cooper knew me.

You've got to combine mechanical ability, physical qualifications and a whole lot of head-work and knowledge of the other fellow to make your third base work most successful.

CHAPTER VI

PLAY IT SAFE IN BASEBALL

As Told to Mitchell V. Charnley

BY

Tristram ("Tris") Speaker

CENTERFIELDER

ONE of the first things I did after I "came up" to the Boston Red Sox from the minor leagues was chase fungoes from the bat of Cy Young, one of the greatest twirlers who ever threw a baseball.

Young used to have a passion for hitting fungoes whenever he wasn't in fielding practice, or pitching to batters. I think it was the first afternoon I was on the field that he called to me.

"Say, youngster," he shouted, "get out there in the field and catch a few flies."

Out I went, mighty glad of every chance I could get to show the club managers and the other players what I could do. I guess I started by playing pretty deep, for it wasn't long before Young was giving me hints about coming closer to the infield.

"Learn to play in and go back for the longer flies," he advised me. Best advice I ever had.

For Young kept hitting fungoes, and I kept developing the close-in style of outfielding. It's a style that's considered mighty effective nowadays, and every boy who wants to be an outfielder ought to study and practice it.

That was late in the 1907 season—I was less than twenty years old—and I only got into three games. The next year I was back with the Little Rock, Arkansas, team. But I didn't forget what Young had told me—that the closer I got to second the better off I'd be. And in August, 1908, I went up to Boston again. That time I stayed. My work with Young kept right on.

If you're practicing for the outfield, learn this close-in style.

Play just as close as you can with safety, and go back to take flies. You should be able to start back just as easily as you start forward. Sounds hard at first, doesn't it? Practice will make it simple, though; the crack of the bat will be a signal to you to whirl and start toward the place the ball's headed for, after you've learned the trick of it.

A mighty good way to start this running-back practice is to have some one hit fungoes to you, as Cy Young did to me. Don't try to come in too much at first. Make it about halfway from the place where you've been playing to the position you expect to reach eventually. When you find you can take the few steps to the rear, turn in plenty of time and get set to catch the ball in front of you, then you're ready to shift your position a little farther forward. In time you will find a position that is close enough to the infield so that you can back up plays well, or dash in and scoop up some of the Texas leaguers that would go for hits if you had been back farther. And you'll still be far enough back to run to the rear, when necessary, and catch the longer flies.

You know of Clyde Milan, once a Washington outfielder? He was a man who improved his playing a whole lot by developing into a close-in fielder. Never tried it before he came to the big leagues. But when he learned it thoroughly, he was twice as effective a player.

Always remember this—try to make catches look easy. Eddie Roush, the great Cincinnati outfielder, is known for the simplicity and smoothness of his play. That's a part of his greatness. Roush never tries to make a sensational catch if an easy catch is possible. He knows that he's flirting with disaster—maybe an extra run, or a lost ball game—if he takes any chances that aren't necessary. Babe Ruth makes 'em look mighty easy, too, as do Jamieson of Cleveland and Ira Flagstead, Red Sox outfielder, and Eddie Collins, Chicago second baseman.

Making chances *look* easy, of course, means actually making them easy. It means getting set to take the ball squarely in front of you whenever you can. It means cupping your hands in front of your body, palms up, instead of trying to catch the ball above your head, or over a shoulder. Once in a while circus catches like these are necessary; every player ought to be able to make them if he has to. But the best player is the one who has the fewest of them to his credit.

Another thing to practice is judging the ball. You'll find that the crack of the ball as it leaves the bat will tell you a good deal about the direction of it's going, and how far you'll have to get back to handle it. You won't have much time to watch its flight, for you start the moment you hear the crack; so judgment is mighty important.

Don't think, because you can't do it the first time, that you're not cut out to be an outfielder. Charlie Jamieson, Cleveland left fielder, looked like anything but a good prospect when he first came up from the minors. He couldn't hit; he couldn't field; he couldn't do anything but pitch a little. The Philadelphia Athletics had already tried him and decided that he wouldn't do.

But Jamieson wanted to play baseball, and had confidence that he could make a good player out of himself. He was never on the bench. He practiced by the hour, fielding and batting, batting and fielding. Whenever anybody was knocking flies out Jamieson was there shagging them. He learned to take a ball properly, to race back when he saw a long fly heading his way, to throw and to bat.

And he made himself into one of the greatest fielders of baseball.

The three outfield positions demand pretty much the same kind of playing. The center-fielder can play a little closer to the infield than the other two. He has more ground to cover, in general, than they have, and so gets more benefit from playing close.

He also backs up more plays than right or left fielder. Every good outfielder can find a definite position for himself on every ball that's hit; Eddie Roush is one of the fielders who never considers himself out of a play. But the center-fielder has two men—second baseman and short-stop—to back up, and the other fielders have one only.

It's mighty important for a player to be sure he's in the right position. I saw a game of high school teams one spring in which the fielders of one nine didn't move a muscle except when they say a ball coming. No matter whether the batter was right or left-handed, whether he had already slugged liners down the left field foul line or to the right fence, they held their places.

That's bad baseball.

There's a different position for every batter. The thing every player on a baseball nine must be able to do is figure, from the way a batsman makes his first swing at a ball, what direction and how hard he's likely to hit. If he takes a full swing, a bit early, he'll probably hit a long one to left field. If he takes that full swing, but more slowly, the ball will head for right field. If he chops, there's more question about it. But usually you can tell pretty well.

The minute he's given you an indication, shift your position to meet the situation. If he's been at bat before, you likely will know something definite about him—that he hits low liners, or ground balls, or long high fouls. Whatever it is, don't let him catch you napping. If you're in a position to meet his weakness, you'll likely catch him out. But if you don't watch the signs, you're not playing your best game.

Don't forget that the speed of your pitcher, particularly if the batter facing him is inexperienced, or has been accustomed to slow-ball pitching, has a lot to do with the direction a hit is going to take. A right-hander who bats against fast pitching is more likely to hit to right field than left, if he hasn't been used to having them served up with lots of speed. . . . But that same man, after he's been to bat once or twice and has had a chance to readjust himself to the fast pitching, may hit to left field—don't forget that, either, or fail to watch for the signs.

The lively ball that was in use for several years

made it more difficult for an outfielder to play close to the infield. I had to shift back a good many feet, after the new ball went in use. Throws to the plate by outfielders became less frequent, too. That's because the ball was usually too far from the plate to give the fielder much chance to catch a runner tearing in from third. But any fielder should plan on preventing a runner from going from first to third on a single. It's much worse for a man to go to third from first than it is for him to steal second, because the minute he gets on third he's in a position to score on almost any kind of a hit, or bunt, or error, or long fly. So don't neglect your throwing arm.

Incidentally, you ought to remember that the big job of an outfielder is catching flies. If an outfielder can't throw, but is a dead-sure trap for any fly that comes to his territory, he's a mighty valuable man. So work on that part of your job all the time.

Here's a bit of strategy that we've used on the Cleveland club with fine effect: pitch to a batter's strength, when the outfield has long enough fences to make it safe. We know that some players usually hit inside curves far into left field. So instead of giving them balls they don't want, we feed them inside curves and let them hit just the way they like to do. Meanwhile our outfielders have all shifted to the left and play deep, so we're all set for the ball we're almost sure they'll send our way.

Some men you can't play in that manner. Babe Ruth, for instance, is a dead right field hitter, and with the many short right field fences we can't afford to feed him the kind of ball he likes. He'd get too many home runs! So the Cleveland pitchers "work on him" and try to give him things he can neither pull for long flies to left center and centerfield, nor whale over the right field fence. Ruth and some of the other hitters haven't any weaknesses, really; so in their cases the pitchers have to depend more on their own skill and less on the fact that the outfielders are in the right positions.

Now, about the best thing any team can do before a game is the thing that all big league teams do, and mighty few others—that's hold a meeting to outline a plan of action. While our opponents are having batting practice on the field, we all gather in the club house and go carefully over the batting list of the other team. The strength and weakness of each regular, as well as any probable pinch hitters, are talked over, and the right way to play for them is suggested. So when we go on the field we know pretty well what we're going to do.

Boys playing on amateur teams would have even more to gain from meetings like these than older players. They would get the specific knowledge they might need for the game they're about to play. And they would acquire the habit of figuring each new batter, or situation, out, and playing for the man or the case as seems wisest.

I've said that the big job of a fielder is to field. That's true, and there has been more than one player carried on a team simply because of his great ability in defense. But the most valuable outfielder, of course, is the man who can hit as well as field. Men like Ruth, and Cobb, and Roush, and Jamieson, and the Meusel brothers, are great because they are stars at both branches of the game.

So every boy player ought to give a lot of his time to batting practice.

Walter Gerber, shortstop of the St. Louis Browns, was just about the worst looking hitter I ever saw when he came to the American League. We could always figure that, when he came to bat, he'd strike out. He simply couldn't connect with the ball. He was a great fielder—one of the best shortstops of recent years—but he was a dead loss in the batting order.

Well, Gerber took himself in hand, for every man has to be his own doctor, pretty much, in baseball. Gerber practiced incessantly. He was always getting some pitcher to go to the bull pen in a corner of the field with him, and George Sisler, great first baseman and batter, to watch him and coach him, and he'd swing a bat by the hour.

Gradually his eye became true, and his timing improved. Before long other teams noticed that Gerber was getting a hit now and then. At last he was just as much to be reckoned with as any other man on the club—and it was all because he worked and practiced and batted until he'd overcome his weaknesses.

Timing and keeping your eye on the ball are the two great things about batting. Never look away from that little white sphere as it's served up to you by the pitcher. If you do lose sight of it for the slightest instant, you've just about lost all chance of connecting. You can't swing your bat in the right line to meet the ball, or shift it with the jump of a curve, if you're not watching it like a hawk.

Timing means swinging your bat so that it meets the ball at exactly the proper moment to get direction as well as distance. If you swing too early, you're going to hit too much to the left; too late, and the ball will angle off to the right. Swinging too hard is another form of poor timing. Practice is the sole remedy for any fault in batting. The first thing to do is learn, by practice, what form is most natural for *you*. I don't believe that any player should be forced to adopt a batting form that seems to tie him in knots. He'll do his best work if he's doing it naturally. Then, as long as he's getting results, he doesn't need to change. But if the hits aren't coming, he'll want to experiment. Joe Sewell, Cleveland shortstop, wasn't bringing in his share of base bingles several years ago. He found he was swinging his bat too hard; so he choked up a bit—that is, gripped the bat a little higher—and cut down the swing. Almost immediately his average began to mount.

When I was first in the big leagues I learned to choke my bat, but for a different reason. I was a dead left field hitter, and I soon found that outfielders knew just exactly where to play for me. That wouldn't do. So I moved my left hand just three or four inches up the bat, and found that I was able to pull the ball around to the right whenever I wanted to. That gave me batting variation, prevented the other team from camping right in the path of my long hits, and boosted my percentage.

Mighty few big league players have the trick of stepping away from the ball that is common among boys. "Stepping away" means bringing the left foot, if you're a right-handed batter, away from the plate as you get set for your swing, instead of straight forward. It's easy to see that you lose force by this backward step; if you step forward, however, you're simply meeting the ball more squarely.

In this as in other batting tricks, I say that the most natural form is the thing for any player to follow. As a rule I don't advise stepping back; but if a player finds it's the easiest way for him to get hits, it's the thing for him to do. Larry Lajoie, the great second baseman of a few years ago, used both forms. On some balls he stepped forward; on others his foot went back. But Lajoie had tremendous strength in his arms, and didn't need the added force he could get by the forward step.

Most fellows make a bad mistake when they try to learn to bat from both sides of the plate. If you're good on right-hand batting, you'd better stick to it and forget batting from the left. It's the old question of using the form that's most natural to you. It'll be easier and, nine times out of ten, more effective.

Of course, some players bat from both sides of the plate—right side against right-handers, and left side against southpaws—but often they've been forced to learn two styles by some definite weakness. Donie Bush, the speedy little short-stop who used to play with Detroit in the Tigers' championship days, could hit left-handers well enough batting right-handed, but he couldn't touch fellows who pitched with their right arms. So he set to work and learned to bunt from the other side of the plate. He became a mighty clever bunter, and with his speed was a danger-ous man. . . . That was a case where knowledge of both styles overcame a fault in a man's play.

Unless there's as good a reason as that, though, a batter ought to stick to the easiest way.

Everybody knows that when the baseball season opens, in the spring, muscles have to be worked into condition gradually. The same thing is true of your batting eye, your timing and everything else. You'll want to start swinging easily at medium-speed pitching—just the kind of pitching that a twirler who hasn't been using his arm all winter will want to serve up. By accustoming yourself to hitting slow balls you'll work your timing and your batting eye into running order again. Then, as the season gets along, the pitcher's speed will be greater and you'll be ready to hit it. This medium speed ball is the best developing practice there is for a batter.

It's the thing to work on if you're in a batting slump, too. The minute you find you've lost your batting eye, or that you don't swing right, take a pitcher into a corner and get him throwing balls of medium speed to you. Keep this up right along, never bothering about fast pitching, until you're able to do what you want to with slow. Then you're ready to start in on more difficult balls again.

Another thing. Don't worry if you find you're in a slump. Harry Heilmann, the slugging Detroit outfielder, one summer worried himself out of the greatest batting average he'd ever collected. Through the early months of the season he could hit anything—was batting above .500. Then he had a minor operation, somewhat similar to the trouble that caused George Sisler to spend a season on the bench. Baseball writers speculated at length as to whether the operation would affect Heilmann's batting, and of course this worried Heilmann.

When he returned to the game the big fielder was in as good condition as he'd ever been. But he couldn't hit. His slump lasted for months, and took his average to a figure that, for Heilmann, was mighty low. . . . And dozens of baseball players talking about the slump, told me that they hadn't a doubt it was worry that caused it. So don't let Old Man Worry get hold of you.

The one thing every boy who wants to be a baseball player of any merit ought to realize is that he's got to learn things for himself. He can't sit on the bench and absorb batting ability, or learn to field a fly by hearing other players talk about it. He's got to be on the jump—just like Jamieson was. Cy Young would never have wanted to help me, I'm mighty sure, if I hadn't showed him I was eager to learn. But the minute a chap gets out and handles a bat or baseball at every opportunity, and shags flies and chases grounders without being told to do it, he's going to find somebody who will give him the hints he needs.

PLAY IT SAFE IN BASEBALL

So that's the formula—do it yourself without being told. Work on the things you need to know most every chance you get. Then, when somebody who *knows*—and in every school or town or playfield there is somebody with a good working knowledge of baseball—gives you some hints, try them out. And some morning you'll wake up and find you can handle a fly, or hit one, a good deal better than the fellow who's done nothing but camp on the bench.